This book is a

Gift

From

....

To

....

Date

....

May God bless you through this book

PRAYERS FOR OVERCOMING ATTITUDE PROBLEMS

PRAYERS FOR OVERCOMING ATTITUDE PROBLEMS

PRAYER M. MADUEKE

Prayer Publications

PRAYER PUBLICATIONS
1 Babatunde close, Off Olaitan Street,
Surulere, Lagos, Nigeria
+234 803 353 0599

PRAYERS FOR OVERCOMING ATTITUDE PROBLEMS

Copyright © 2013

PRAYER M. MADUEKE

ISBN: 9781492917564

Prayer Publications

First Edition, 2013

For further information of permission

1 Babatunde close, off Olaitan Street, Surulere, Lagos, Nigeria

+234 803 353 0599
Email: pastor@prayermadueke.com,
Website: www.prayermadueke.com

Table of Contents

COMPREHENSIVE PRAYER LIST

DEDICATION

This book is dedicated to individuals and families, who are sincerely trusting God for His Spirit of wisdom to live good Christian lives according to His Word.

"Then they cry unto the LORD in their trouble, and he saveth them out of their distresses. He sent his word, and healed them, and delivered them from their destructions" (<u>Psalms 107:19-20</u>).

PERSONAL DELIVERANCE

CHAPTER OVERVIEW

- The command to cast out demons
- The ministry of the devil
- How to conduct personal deliverance

"[1]After these things the Lord appointed other seventy also, and sent them two and two before his face into every city and place, whither he himself would come…. [18]And he said unto them, I beheld Satan as lightning fall from heaven. [19]Behold, I give unto you power to tread on serpents and scorpions, and over all the power of the enemy: and nothing shall by any means hurt you. [20]Notwithstanding in this rejoice not, that the spirits are subject unto you; but rather rejoice, because your names are written in heaven" (Luke 10:1, 18-20).

And English dictionary defined deliverance as *the action of being rescued or set free*. While this definition is true, I will seek to expound on the concept of personal deliverance in this book; a concept many Christians are yet not familiar with.

When Jesus gave every born-again Christian the power to tread on serpents and scorpions, and over all the power of the enemy, He invited all believers to the ministry of deliverance. Therefore, individual believers, who exercise their authority in the Word of God, can understand that personal deliverance is simply a ministration of deliverance by every believer.

A deliverance minister is one who deals with his or her problems first by applying the Word, before seeking for help elsewhere. It is a decisive effort by an individual at a definite time to pray and set him or herself free from a particular problem or attack. Believers ought to be experts in personal deliverance. This helps born-again Christians to strengthen their faith in Christ and trust God for greater exploits.

THE COMMAND TO CAST OUT DEMONS

Christ commanded all believers to cast out demons in His name and heal the sick. That's why the practice of personal deliverance brings good results to your life and lives of others around you. As a believer, you have been empowered to cast out demons from your personal life, business, job, family, and anywhere you see devil operate.

> *"16He that believeth and is baptized shall be saved; but he that believeth not shall be damned. 17And these signs shall follow them that believe; In my name shall they cast out devils; they shall speak with new tongues; 18They shall take up serpents; and if they drink any deadly thing, it shall not hurt them; they shall lay hands on the sick, and they shall recover"* (Mark 16:16-18).

Unfortunately, most Christians are not aware that as soon as they became born-again Christians, they were empowered to do the ministry of deliverance by preaching to themselves first, and then others, and commanding evil spirits to leave.

The moment you repented, confessed and forsook your sins, you received the power to stop or dislodge demonic activities anywhere you see them. In fact, as a born-again Christian, Jesus empowered you to tread on demons and nothing can hurt you by any means. A believer's power is made manifest through prayers. As a believer, you can do the work of deliverance even more than Christ had time to do while on earth. You can do all things through Christ Jesus, who strengthens you. You can achieve a lot through prayers, including complete personal deliverance.

> *"12Verily, verily, I say unto you, He that believeth on me, the works that I do shall he do also; and greater works than these shall he do; because I go unto my Father. 13And whatsoever ye shall ask in my name, that will I do, that the Father may be glorified in the*

Son. ¹⁴If ye shall ask any thing in my name, I will do it" (<u>John 14:12-14</u>).

"¹⁸Verily I say unto you, Whatsoever ye shall bind on earth shall be bound in heaven: and whatsoever ye shall loose on earth shall be loosed in heaven" (<u>Matthew 18:18</u>).

"¹And as Jesus passed by, he saw a man which was blind from his birth" (<u>John 9:1</u>).

It is very difficult, and almost impossible, to go through personal deliverance without believing in Christ and His Word. Prayers without trust in God's Word can produce witchcraft results. Witchcraft results are capable of attracting demons into people's lives, prolonging their activities and cannot cast out evil spirits. They are capable of bringing counterfeit results or fake deliverance.

"⁷For the mystery of iniquity doth already work: only he who now letteth will let, until he be taken out of the way. ⁸And then shall that Wicked be revealed, whom the Lord shall consume with the spirit of his mouth, and shall destroy with the brightness of his coming: ⁹Even him, whose coming is after the working of Satan with all power and signs and lying wonders, ¹⁰And with all deceivableness of unrighteousness in them that perish; because they received not the love of the truth, that they might be saved. ¹¹And for this cause God shall send them strong delusion, that they should believe a lie: ¹²That they all might be damned who believed not the truth, but had pleasure in unrighteousness" (<u>2 Thessalonians 2:7-12</u>).

It is also dangerous to ignore the practice of personal deliverance. People, who do, often fall victims of deliverance without Christ being the deliverer and the source of deliverance. Satanic deliverance ministers can transfer evil spirits from your leg to the head or from your body to your business, work, children, or even prolong demonic attacks in your life.

"¹⁹There was a certain rich man, which was clothed in purple and fine linen, and fared sumptuously every day: ²⁰And there was a certain beggar named Lazarus, which was laid at his gate, full of sores, ²¹And desiring to be fed with the crumbs which fell from the rich man's table: moreover the dogs came and licked his sores. ²²And it came to pass, that the beggar died, and was carried by the angels into Abraham's bosom: the rich man also died, and was buried; ²³And in hell he lift up his eyes, being in torments, and seeth Abraham afar off, and Lazarus in his bosom. ²⁴And he cried and said, Father Abraham, have mercy on me, and send Lazarus, that he may dip the tip of his finger in water, and cool my tongue; for I am tormented in this flame. ²⁵But Abraham said, Son, remember that thou in thy lifetime receivedst thy good things, and likewise Lazarus evil things: but now he is comforted, and thou art tormented. ²⁶And beside all this, between us and you there is a great gulf fixed: so that they, which would pass from hence to you, cannot; neither can they pass to us that would come from thence. ²⁷Then he said, I pray thee therefore, father, that thou wouldest send him to my father's house: ²⁸For I have five brethren; that he may testify unto them, lest they also come into this place of torment. ²⁹Abraham saith unto him, They have Moses and the prophets; let them hear them. ³⁰And he said, Nay, father Abraham: but if one went unto them from the dead, they will repent. ³¹And he said unto him, If they hear not Moses and the prophets, neither will they be persuaded, though one rose from the dead" (<u>Luke 16:19-31</u>).

The mystery of iniquity can enable a sinner, a native doctor, an occult person, a very wicked unbeliever or immoral person to transfer sicknesses from place to place, person to person instead of casting them out completely. That's why it is very important for every believer to study the Bible and be conversant with the Word of God because knowledge of the Word is the greatest instrument of deliverance. Your exploits in the Word while praying and the use of Christ's name are very effective weapon for true deliverance.

"[30]As he spake these words, many believed on him. [31]Then said Jesus to those Jews, which believed, on him, If ye continue in my word, then are ye my disciples indeed; [32]And ye shall know the truth, and the truth shall make you free. [36]If the Son therefore shall make you free, ye shall be free indeed" (John 8:30-32, 36).

"[21]Not every one that saith unto me, Lord, Lord, shall enter into the kingdom of heaven; but he that doeth the will of my Father which is in heaven. [22]Many will say to me in that day, Lord, Lord, have we not prophesied in thy name? And in thy name have cast out devils? And in thy name done many wonderful works? [23]And then will I profess unto them, I never knew you: depart from me, ye that work iniquity" (Matthew 7:21-23).

It is very disappointing to let you know that many deliverance ministries on earth lack the knowledge of God's Word. Yet the same ministers are specialists in prayers that do not have reference to the Holy Spirit. As a result, they produce counterfeit results and deceptive miracles and wonders. Some of these ministers preach the Word of God very well but lack the evidence of fruits of the spirit and are equally failures in practical Christian living.

However, most of them have been successful in concealing their true characters. But when you encounter them, you discover that even with their voluminous good teachings, they are swindlers and cheats. Most of them, who started really well, have deviated from the faith, having surrounded themselves with liars and carnal minded advisers and followers. That's why in their real lives, they have backslidden and are not aware that the Lord has departed from them.

"[20]And she said, The Philistines be upon thee, Samson. And he awoke out of his sleep, and said, I will go out as at other times before, and shake myself. And he wist not that the LORD was departed from him" (Judges 16:20).

Determine this day to start practicing the art of personal deliverance. The devil effectively using so many backslidden deliverance ministers, who appear like angels of God but are very wicked and destructive (*See* Exodus 7:10-13, 20-22, 8:5-7, 20-23, 1 Samuel 18:10-11, Ezekiel 9:1-4, Revelation 13:11-17, 2 Corinthians 11:13-15, Matthew 7:15).

When you encounter fake deliverance ministers, it is easy to notice their greed, pride, anger, immorality, covetousness, jealousy, financial irresponsibility, unfaithfulness to their families and wickedness. That's why it is very important to become born-again first before giving yourself in to deliverance. Another important thing you have to ensure is that your uttermost commitment must be to Christ and His Word, not only to the church or to ministers. When you became saved, you gave your life to Christ, not to the church or the person that prayed for your salvation or deliverance. Unfortunately, many Christians have missed this part of their commitment.

Equally, fellowship with brethren or believers is very important but should not choke or replace your sincere commitment to Christ. In the believer's gathering, you can be prayed for but not contrary to God's Word (*See* Acts 4:19-20, Matthew 18:18-20, Hebrews 10:25, Acts 4:32-37). A fellow believer or minister can help you in personal deliverance but the Word of God must be the integral part of the deliverance.

> *"⁶The husbandman that labored must be first partaker of the fruits. ⁷Consider what I say; and the Lord give thee understanding in all things...¹⁹ Nevertheless the foundation of God standeth sure, having this seal, The Lord knoweth them that are his. And, Let everyone that nameth the name of Christ depart from iniquity. ²⁰But in a great house there are not only vessels of gold and of silver, but also of wood and of earth; and some to honor, and some to dishonor. ²¹If a man therefore purge himself from these, he shall be a vessel unto honor, sanctified, and meet for the master's use, and prepared unto every good work... ⁵Having a form of*

godliness, but denying the power thereof: from such turn away" (2 Timothy 2:6-7, 19-21, 3:5).

To be able to conduct deliverance upon yourself and others, you must have assurance of your salvation and have boldness in God's Word. You ought to be bold when you are determined to approach the throne of God in order to confront devil and the hosts of his kingdom.

"¹⁹Now therefore ye are no more strangers and foreigners, but fellow citizens with the saints, and of the household of God; ²⁰And are built upon the foundation of the apostles and prophets, Jesus Christ himself being the chief corner stone" (Ephesians 2:19-20).

Being ignorant of who you are in Christ is capable of limiting your boldness and holding you back from victory over devil. You cannot afford to rely on experienced believers and gifted ministers all the time. If you are born-again, then you ought to minister deliverance to yourself.

"²And he sent Eliakim, who was over the household, and Shebna the scribe, and the elders of the priests covered with sackcloth, unto Isaiah the prophet the son of Amoz. ³And they said unto him, Thus saith Hezekiah, This day is a day of trouble, and of rebuke, and of blasphemy: for the children are come to the birth, and there is not strength to bring forth. ⁴It may be the LORD thy God will hear the words of Rabshakeh, whom the king of Assyria his master hath sent to reproach the living God, and will reprove the words which the LORD thy God hath heard: wherefore lift up thy prayer for the remnant that is left... ¹In those days was Hezekiah sick unto death. And Isaiah the prophet the son of Amoz came unto him, and said unto him, Thus saith the LORD, Set thine house in order: for thou shalt die, and not live. ²Then Hezekiah turned his face toward the wall, and prayed unto the LORD, ³And said, Remember now, O LORD, I beseech thee, and how I have walked before thee in truth and with a perfect heart, and have done that

which is good in thy sight. And Hezekiah wept sore"
(Isaiah 38:1-3, 37:2-4).

In order to deliver yourself and others effectively, you must be born-again and know your rights and benefits in Christ. Every believer has gained a new relationship with Christ, which is highly potential. When Moses entered into partnership with God, He promised to be with Moses. That was how Moses' deliverance ministry started.

> *"¹¹And Moses said unto God, Who am I, that I should go unto Pharaoh, and that I should bring forth the children of Israel out of Egypt? ¹²And he said, Certainly I will be with thee; and this shall be a token unto thee, that I have sent thee: When thou hast brought forth the people out of Egypt, ye shall serve God upon this mountain"* (Exodus 3:11-12).

> *"¹⁵And he said unto him, Oh my Lord, wherewith shall I save Israel? Behold, my family is poor in Manasseh, and I am the least in my father's house. ¹⁶And the LORD said unto him, Surely I will be with thee, and thou shalt smite the Midianites as one man"* (Judges 6:15-16).

The problem with many believers is that they relate with their circumstances and conclude that God is not really with them. That's why doubt, unbelief and ignorance of divine presence are great obstacle to deliverance. No matter how poor you are or your family background, once you are born-again, God empowers you to be able to conduct deliverance.

Poverty defeated Gideon, who later became a national deliverer, while his family suffered from extreme lack. God promised you, as a believer, His divine presence. He would not allow His children to fight against unclean spirits on their own. God does the battle for His people.

> *"⁵Let your conversation be without covetousness; and be content with such things as ye have: for he hath said, I will never leave thee, nor forsake thee. ⁶So that we may boldly say, The Lord is my helper, and I will*

not fear what man shall do unto me" (<u>Hebrews 13:5-6</u>).

The Lord is your help, and no power of darkness can have victory over you. No matter how young you are as a Christian, when you know your right, you can boldly face the enemy and overcome him anywhere you meet him. It is an insult for you to allow the devil to waste your life because you are not an outcast, slave or a stranger in the house of God, your Father.

According to Scriptures, you are a legitimate son and child of God. Therefore, it is a sin for you to underestimate yourself or your God.

> *"¹⁴For as many as are led by the Spirit of God, they are the sons of God"* (<u>Romans 8:14</u>).

> *"⁵To redeem them that were under the law, that we might receive the adoption of sons"* (<u>Galatians 4:5</u>).

> *"¹⁵Of whom the whole family in heaven and earth is named"* (<u>Ephesians 3:15</u>).

When you value yourself rightly, believing that you are who God said you are, then deliver yourself from any satanic bondage that is tormenting your life. True Christians, who know whom they are in Christ, do not accept defeat by devil.

> *"¹⁸And I say also unto thee, That thou art Peter, and upon this rock I will build my church; and the gates of hell shall not prevail against it"* (<u>Matthew 16:18</u>).

> *"³⁰For we are members of his body, of his flesh, and of his bones"* (<u>Ephesians 5:30</u>).

You are a member of the body of Christ and it is not right for you to allow the devil to oppress Christ's body. Even when devil attacks you, if you would resist him courageously, the gates of hell cannot prevail. You belong to the heavenly family of God.

It is equally dangerous to ignore the devil. You must resist him. Otherwise, he is committed to fulfilling his ministry on earth. You need to resist his works in your life, before he harvests your life.

> *"⁷Submit yourselves therefore to God. Resist the devil, and he will flee from you"* (James 4:7).

> *"⁸Be sober, be vigilant; because your adversary the devil, as a roaring lion, walketh about, seeking whom he may devour: ⁹Whom resist steadfast in the faith, knowing that the same afflictions are accomplished in your brethren that are in the world"* (1 Peter 5:8-9).

If you are waiting for someone to do all the prayers and deliverance for you, you may be shocked to discover that no one would do that for you. That's why many Christians do not experience true freedom in their Christian lives.

THE MINISTRY OF THE DEVIL

One of the greatest hindrances in deliverance is not being able to discern the difference between the work of devil and the work of God. Many people misinterpret devil's work to be God's work. Where this error existed, it is hard to resist the devil. While many Christians remain complacent, hoping that devil would someday give up on his own, others believe that once they are Christians, they don't need to pray anymore because God has delivered them already.

Many Christians are watching the devil fulfill his ministry in the lives of others and theirs as well. This is wrong and cannot be entertained. Works of the devil must be recognized and resisted at all cost. I have listed a few of the ministry, works and office of the devil to help you identify them:

The devil causes divorce and remarriage (See Malachi 2:11-17).

He influences people, leaders or his agents to decree against God's children (See Exodus 3:1-15).

He forces people to serve the queen of heaven, idolatry (See Jeremiah 44:15-18).

He raises people to promote apostasy (See 1 Timothy 4:1-3).

He frustrates uncompromising victims (See Jeremiah 44:15-18).

He makes people to inquire from idols (See 2 Kings 1:1-18).

He deceives God's children to become covetous, tell lies and refuse to repent (See 2 Kings 5:20-27).

He pushes God's children into compromises (See 1 Kings 22:1-50)

He threatens the lives of God's prophets (See 1 Kings 19:1-3).

He attacks God's children, prophets and causes them to backslide (See 1 Kings 13:11-32)

He attacks people with barrenness (See 1 Samuel 1:6, 19-20, 24-28, 2:1-11, 20-21)

He destroys ministers' children with sin (See 1 Samuel 2:12-17).

He promotes poverty in the lives of God's children (See Luke 16:20-22).

He delays people from discovering their destiny on time.

He makes people's lives useless by attacking them with deaf and dumb spirits (See Matthew 9:32-33)

He attacks people with lunacy and mania (See Matthew 4:24, 17:14-21, Mark 5:1-18).

He makes people to become tired of living and to commit suicide (See Matthew 17:15, Mark 5:1-18)

He brings people from birth to death (See John 9:1-3, 6-9).

He vexes people's lives with grievous torments (See Matthew 15:22).

He attacks people with all manner of sickness and diseases (See Matthew 4:23-25).

He paralyzes people's body organs (See Matthew 8:5-13).

He fills people's bodies with unclean spirits (See Mark 1:23-29).

He attacks households of God's ministers (See Mark 1:30-31).

He destroys people's handiworks (See Mark 3:1-5)

He attacks people with demonic plagues and unclean spirits (See Mark 3:1-11).

He kills people without mercy (See Mark 5:25-34)

He causes people to toil in life without success (See Luke 5:1-11).

He kills people prematurely (See Luke 7:11-17).

He causes people to be mad (See Luke 8:26-39*).*

He keeps people in bounds for life (See Luke 13:11-13*)*

He renders some people impotent (See John 5:1-9*).*

He moves God's children to tell lies (See Genesis 18:9-15*).*

He brings strife among brethren (See Genesis 13:7-8*).*

He put believers in prison (See Acts 4:1-5*).*

He incites people to insult Christ (See Matthew 27:38-44, 27:48-50*).*

He brings lust into the congregation (See Numbers 11*).*

The devil is the source all sicknesses and afflictions. He uses the weapon of sin to take over people's lives. He entices people to consult him for palm reading, fortune telling, magic, witchcraft, etc.

> *"14Afterward Jesus findeth him in the temple, and said unto him, Behold, thou art made whole: sin no more, lest a worse thing come unto thee"* (John 5:14).

> *"14But the Spirit of the LORD departed from Saul, and an evil spirit from the LORD troubled him. 15And Saul's servants said unto him, Behold now, an evil spirit from God troubleth thee"* (1 Samuel 16:14-15).

> *"27Neither give place to the devil"* (Ephesians 4:27).

> *"44Then he saith, I will return into my house from whence I came out; and when he is come, he findeth it empty, swept, and garnished. 45Then goeth he, and taketh with himself seven other spirits more wicked than himself, and they enter in and dwell there: and the last state of that man is worse than the first. Even so shall it be also unto this wicked generation"* (Matthew 12:44-45)

If you have practiced idolatry in the past, or opened your heart to occult practices, or committed grievous sins, then it is possible devil took advantage of your past. In that case, you may need deliverance. And if you still have satanic properties like charms, staffs, occult materials, etc., in your possession, it means devil is still very much around with you. Repent truthfully for your deliverance to be perfected. Then destroy all satanic properties in your possession and abandon all evil lifestyles you lived in the past, before you begin these prayers of deliverance.

> *"³And Samuel spake unto all the house of Israel, saying, If ye do return unto the LORD with all your hearts, then put away the strange gods and Ashtaroth from among you, and prepare your hearts unto the LORD, and serve him only: and he will deliver you out of the hand of the Philistines. ⁴Then the children of Israel did put away Baalim and Ashtaroth, and served the LORD only"* (1 Samuel 7:3-4).

> *"¹⁸And many that believed came, and confessed, and shewed their deeds. ¹⁹Many of them also which used curious arts brought their books together, and burned them before all men: and they counted the price of them, and found it fifty thousand pieces of silver"* (Acts 19:18-19).

In addition, I like to mention another type of deliverance, which I call mass deliverance. This is a concerted effort by any deliverance ministry to proclaim Jesus Christ to an entire group of people, who need deliverance. These are seemingly multitudes of people, who are bound, afflicted, oppressed, bruised and imprisoned by the devil. They are mainly sinners, sick and poor people and people under attacks. While some are in dire need of healing and deliverance, others need salvation, abundant life, freedom from sin and frustrations. Without complete deliverance, people go through repeated circles of failure, fear and oppression. And this is exactly why Jesus came; to deliver the oppress and set captives free.

"³⁸ How God anointed Jesus of Nazareth with the Holy Ghost and with power: who went about doing good, and healing all that were oppressed of the devil; for God was with Him" (<u>Acts 10:38</u>).

Jesus was very involved in mass deliverance. He went about doing good and healing all that were oppressed of the devil. Some other times, He conducted deliverance one on one.

HOW TO CONDUCT PERSONAL DELIVERANCE

To deliver yourself, you have to make sure that you confess all your sins and determine to forsake them. You have to be sincere with God, trusting Him to help you not to return to sins you repented of and confessed.

> *"[13]He that covereth his sins shall not prosper: but whoso confesseth and forsaketh them shall have mercy"* ([Proverbs 28:13](#)).

> *"[7]Be not deceived; God is not mocked: for whatsoever a man soweth, that shall he also reap. [8]For he that soweth to his flesh shall of the flesh reap corruption; but he that soweth to the Spirit shall of the Spirit reap life everlasting"* ([Galatians 6:7-8](#)).

No one can deceive God. He knows when you are sincere and when you are insincere. Promising God absolute obedience without determining sincerely to live for God is self-deceit and mockery of the divinity of God. You must be mindful also that every promise and confession made to God can be tested or tried before real and lasting answers from God come.

> *"[14]Afterward Jesus findeth him in the temple, and said unto him, Behold, thou art made whole: sin no more, lest a worse thing come unto thee... [11]She said, No man, Lord. And Jesus said unto her, Neither do I condemn thee: go, and sin no more"* ([John 8:11, 5:14](#)).

> *"[13]Every man's work shall be made manifest: for the day shall declare it, because it shall be revealed by fire; and the fire shall try every man's work of what sort it is"* ([1 Corinthians 3:13](#)).

> *"[14]And when Jesus was come into Peter's house, he saw his wife's mother laid, and sick of a fever. [15]And he touched her hand, and the fever left her: and she arose, and ministered unto them"* ([Matthew 8:14-15](#)).

It is foolishness, complete waste of time and invitation to more trouble for you to go for deliverance when you know you are not ready to forsake the sins you are confessing. It causes worst things to happen and prolongs your suffering. If you received freedom at all, it is fake and can be very disastrous. For devil to postpone your suffering in order to allow a temporary deliverance can very destructive and disheartening.

> "²⁴And he cried and said, Father Abraham, have mercy on me, and send Lazarus, that he may dip the tip of his finger in water, and cool my tongue; for I am tormented in this flame. ²⁵But Abraham said, Son, remember that thou in thy lifetime receivedst thy good things, and likewise Lazarus evil things: but now he is comforted, and thou art tormented" (Luke 16:24-25).

Turning away from sin is the most important prerequisite for all deliverance. Sinners, occultists and all rich people without reference to Christ may have their feast days now. But one thing is sure; they cannot have any safe days. Their days are cursed and God's wrath remains upon them. Without true repentance, whatever you are pursuing now or already have cannot deliver you when God's anger descends.

So when you have received Christ as your Lord and Savior, having repented of your sins, and have determined to forsake them, the next thing to do is to approach God with praise, worships and songs of thanksgiving for God's goodness and mercy upon your life. You have to trust God to keep you alive henceforth, and He will deliver you from every problem and hopeless situations.

Then, study God's Word, especially His promises and scriptures that deal with deliverance. These scriptures would remind you of the authority Christ has given you over the devil (*See* Psalms 84:11, Isaiah 49:24-26, Matthew 4:23-24, 8:28-34, 9:32-33, 10:1-8, 12:28-29, 17:14-21, Acts 10:38, Acts 8:5-8, Matthew 18:8, 19, Matthew 12:28-29, Romans 8:11, 1 Corinthians 6:19, Mark 16:17-18, Luke 10:18-20, 9:1,

John 14:12-14, Romans 8:26-27, 1 Corinthians 3:16, Job 33:4, Matthew 10:20).

As a born-again, you have the spirit of God living in you. Therefore, no sickness, problem or evil spirit can stand before the mighty Spirit of God or the name of Christ, which you use.

> *"⁹Wherefore God also hath highly exalted him, and given him a name which is above every name: ¹⁰That at the name of Jesus every knee should bow, of things in heaven, and things in earth, and things under the earth; ¹¹And that every tongue should confess that Jesus Christ is Lord, to the glory of God the Father"* (Philippians 2:9-11).

> *"¹⁰The name of the LORD is a strong tower: the righteous runneth into it, and is safe"* (Proverbs 18:10).

The spirit of God is able to lift you above every other name, problem or Satan. You can enter into covenant of healing by using God's Word against every problem in your life (*See* Exodus 15:26, Psalms 103:3, Proverbs 4:20-22, Isaiah 53:4-5, 54:15-17, Matthew 8:16-17, James 5:14-15, 1 Peter 2:24, Exodus 23:25-31, Deuteronomy 7:12-15, Psalms 105:37, Numbers 21:4-9, 2 Chronicles 30:18-20, Psalms 103:1-5, 107:17-20, Deuteronomy 28:15-29, 58-61, 2 Chronicles 7:14, John 6:63, Romans 10:17, Psalms 91:14-16).

You can also demand for God's deliverance through His mercy (*See* Matthew 20:30-34, Luke 6:36, James 3:17, 5:11).

Also ask God to deliver you through His mighty power (*See* Matthew 28:18-20, Colossians 1:16-17, Matthew 19:26, 2 Chronicles 16:9, Philippians 4:13).

You can use the above guiding scriptures each day of your program. Study God's Words and use them to formulate your prayers. You can insist on returning to God's original purpose for life through prayers.

"²⁶And God said, Let us make man in our image, after our likeness: and let them have dominion over the fish of the sea, and over the fowl of the air, and over the cattle, and over all the earth, and over every creeping thing that creepeth upon the earth. ²⁷So God created man in his own image, in the image of God created he him; male and female created he them. ²⁸And God blessed them, and God said unto them, Be fruitful, and multiply, and replenish the earth, and subdue it: and have dominion over the fish of the sea, and over the fowl of the air, and over every living thing that moveth upon the earth" (Genesis 1:26-28).

You should not allow sickness, problem, pestilence, fever, ulcer, boils, cancer, swellings, itching, madness, heart failure, blindness, plagues, poverty and economic problems to waste your life for any reason. Your knowledge of God's Word is enough to facilitate your deliverance, and is also capable of producing all manner of miracles in your life and prospers you beyond your imagination. God loves you and wants you to be free from problems.

"⁸He that loveth not knoweth not God; for God is love" (1 John 4:8).

"⁷Ask, and it shall be given you; seek, and ye shall find; knock, and it shall be opened unto you: ⁸For every one that asketh receiveth; and he that seeketh findeth; and to him that knocketh it shall be opened. ⁹Or what man is there of you, whom if his son ask bread, will he give him a stone? ¹⁰Or if he asks a fish, will he give him a serpent? ¹¹If ye then, being evil, know how to give good gifts unto your children, how much more shall your Father which is in heaven give good things to them that ask him?" (Matthew 7:7-11).

"¹⁷Every good gift and every perfect gift is from above, and cometh down from the Father of lights, with whom is no variableness, neither shadow of turning" (James 1:17).

"3According as his divine power hath given unto us all things that pertain unto life and godliness, through the knowledge of him that hath called us to glory and virtue: 4Whereby are given unto us exceeding great and precious promises: that by these ye might be partakers of the divine nature, having escaped the corruption that is in the world through lust" (2 Peter 1:3-4).

"19But my God shall supply all your need according to his riches in glory by Christ Jesus" (Philippians 4:19).

"20Now unto him that is able to do exceeding abundantly above all that we ask or think, according to the power that worketh in us" (Ephesians 3:20).

Do not be afraid to ask for great things. It is the nature of God to do great things. Mercy is one of His attributes and divine character. He is gracious, merciful and kind. It is marvelous to know that He has power to do all good things and nothing is impossible before Him, including your deliverance. He is the source and possessor of all power and His power will work for you today. You are free to use God's power in your deliverance exploits. You can use God's dynamic power and authority, which are also His Dunamis power over all evil.

"1Then he called his twelve disciples together, and gave them power and authority over all devils, and to cure diseases. 2And he sent them to preach the kingdom of God, and to heal the sick. 3And he said unto them, Take nothing for your journey, neither staves, nor scrip, neither bread, neither money; neither have two coats apiece. 4And whatsoever house ye enter into, there abide, and thence depart. 5And whosoever will not receive you, when ye go out of that city, shake off the very dust from your feet for a testimony against them. 6And they departed, and went through the towns, preaching the gospel, and healing everywhere. 7Now Herod the tetrarch heard of all that was done by him: and he was perplexed, because that it was said of

some, that John was risen from the dead; ⁸And of some,
that Elias had appeared; and of others, that one of the
old prophets was risen again. ⁹And Herod said, John
have I beheaded: but who is this, of whom I hear such
things? And he desired to see him. ¹⁰And the apostles,
when they were returned, told him all that they had
done. And he took them, and went aside privately into
a desert place belonging to the city called Bethsaida...
¹⁹They answering said, John the Baptist; but some say,
Elias; and others say, that one of the old prophets is
risen again. ²⁰He said unto them, But whom say ye
that I am? Peter answering said, The Christ of God.
²¹And he straitly charged them, and commanded them
to tell no man that thing" (Luke 9:1-10, 19-21).

Finally, before you go into prayer warfare, make a list of all
known problems. Categorize them if you can. This will make
it easy to pray targeted prayer.

Present each of the listed problems to God. Often, prayers
are divided into two categories; talking to God and talking
to your problems or the powers behind them. Make all you
desire from God through this program known to Him in
prayers. You can also make your supplication and uttering
known to Him by crying to Him. Report the devil and his
works in your life to God and appeal for divine intervention.

Call upon the name of the LORD. Pour your whole heart to
God and take time to seek His face in prayers – (*See* Psalms
42:1-2, 63:1-3, 84:2, Exodus 22:23, Psalms 86:3, Isaiah 44:17,
Luke 18:1-7-13, Hosea 14:3, Romans 10:12-14, Lamentations
3:41, 1 Samuel 1:15, Psalms 27:8). Making a list is the first
part, which is also your preparation. The second part is
praying warfare prayers of deliverance.

"¹And Nadab and Abihu, the sons of Aaron, took either of them his censer, and put fire therein, and put incense thereon, and offered strange fire before the LORD, which he commanded them not. ²And there went out fire from the LORD, and devoured them, and they died before the LORD" (Leviticus 10:1-2).

While prayer is communication with the Almighty, prayer warfare is resisting and confronting the devil through intensive prayers until he gives way. Unbelievably, every human on earth is involved in spiritual warfare. But only true Christians achieve complete victory. Confronting Satan while remaining a sinner will be disastrous. You cannot win. That's why you need Jesus Christ in your life as quickly as possible.

Tactically, you need to have good knowledge of spiritual warfare. Otherwise, you may live and die as a loser. For a Christian to live under the mercy of the devil is a disgrace. You are a temple of God. Therefore, no demon or unclean spirit is allowed to defile the temple of God or bring strange fires into God's temple and go free.

When you know the truth, you will be free from all oppressions of the enemy. You cannot fight spiritual warfare with human technique. The only way you can win a spiritual warfare is to fight while clothed with God's armor.

"¹⁰Finally, my brethren, be strong in the Lord, and in the power of his might. ¹¹Put on the whole armor of God that ye may be able to stand against the wiles of the devil. ¹²For we wrestle not against flesh and blood, but against principalities, against powers, against the rulers of the darkness of this world, against spiritual wickedness in high places. ¹³Wherefore take unto you the whole armor of God that ye may be able to withstand in the evil day, and having done all, to stand. ¹⁴Stand therefore, having your loins girt about with truth, and having on the breastplate of righteousness; ¹⁵And your feet shod with the preparation of the gospel of peace; ¹⁶Above all, taking the shield of faith, wherewith ye shall be able to quench

all the fiery darts of the wicked. [17]And take the helmet of salvation, and the sword of the Spirit, which is the word of God: [18]Praying always with all prayer and supplication in the Spirit, and watching thereunto with all perseverance and supplication for all saints" (Ephesians 6:10-18).

Unfortunately, many Christians are spiritually lazy and weak. How could a spiritually weak Christian resist the devil successfully? That's why many Christians have continued to live at the mercy of the devil. This shouldn't be so.

In spiritual warfare, there is need for regular fast. There is also need to keep vigil and pray all through the night. Other times, you may need to wake up before dawn and pray. There is always a price to pay in spiritual warfare.

"[25]When Jesus saw that the people came running together, he rebuked the foul spirit, saying unto him, Thou dumb and deaf spirit, I charge thee, come out of him, and enter no more into him. [26]And the spirit cried, and rent him sore, and came out of him: and he was as one dead; insomuch that many said, He is dead. [27]But Jesus took him by the hand, and lifted him up; and he arose. [28]And when he was come into the house, his disciples asked him privately, Why could not we cast him out? [29]And he said unto them, This kind can come forth by nothing, but by prayer and fasting" (Mark 9:25-29).

You have to learn to trust God, have faith and fast. The Scriptures made it clear that a fervent prayer of a righteous avails much. Your prayers are able to bind and loose satanic bondages. Christians can no longer afford to allow the camp of the devil make gains over God's children.

Likewise, Christians, who ignore spiritual warfare, often pay dearly for their negligence. That's why Paul likened a Christian life to wrestling, fighting and warfare (*See* Ephesians 6:12, 1 Timothy 6:12, 1 Corinthians 9:25-27, 2 Corinthians 10:3-5, 1 Corinthians 15:30-32).

In your spiritual walk, you must not let doubt, fear, discouragement or unbelief rob you of your trust and faith in God. As you go into spiritual warfare, make sure you do not pray against God's revealed will for your life (*See* Mark 11:25-26, Matthew 5:23-26, Psalms 66:18-20, Deuteronomy 1:41-45, Proverbs 1:28-32, 28:9, Proverbs 21:13, Isaiah 1:15, 1 Samuel 8:6-9, Matthew 6:9-10).

With strength, faith and grace you will overcome the devil and reclaim your possessions. God cannot abandon His people, who trust in Him. Separate yourself from sin, tempters and temptress. Shut every channel through which the devil may use to attack your life.

As you pray these prayers, some of what you are going to say will start manifesting physically. When that happens, continue saying your prayers. Even so, some of the demons responsible for your problems will begin to manifest. So you can expect physically manifestations of demons during deliverance.

Make sure you don't rush through your prayers. If you need to vomit, vomit. If you need to shout, yawn, cry, groan, belch, laugh, sigh, weep or command, do it as God leads you. And when you are addressing a particular prayer point and notice that something is beginning to happen, don't rush to the next prayer point. Instead, spend longer time through that particular prayer point until you have completely dealt with that issue.

Finally, I am convinced that God is going to lead you through as you engage in your deliverance session. It is well with you in the name of Jesus – Amen.

PRAYERS FOR DELIVERANCE

1. As I praise, worship and thank God now, let my deliverance manifest, in the name of Jesus.

2. O Lord, I trust in Your Word for my deliverance, in the name of Jesus. (*See* <u>Matthew 8:5-13</u>).

3. Lord Jesus, touch my body for immediate healing and deliverance, in the name of Jesus. (*See* <u>Matthew 8:14-15</u>).

4. Every yoke of ancestral sin in my life, break, in the name of Jesus.

5. I breathe the Holy Ghost fire for my deliverance now, in the name of Jesus.

6. Let the power of the Holy Ghost knock out my problems, in the name of Jesus.

7. Power to obey every command from Jesus Christ, possess me, in the name of Jesus. (*See* <u>Matthew 12:10-13</u>).

8. Every demonic property in my possessions, I destroy you now, in the name of Jesus. (*See* <u>Acts 19:18-19</u>).

9. I plead the blood of Jesus over every problem in my life, in the name of Jesus. (*See* <u>Revelation 12:11</u>).

10. Every covenant keeping me in bondage, break, , in the name of Jesus.

11. I drink the blood of Jesus for my deliverance, in the name of Jesus.

12. I loose myself from satanic bondage, in the name of Jesus.

13. I bind and cast out every evil spirit behind my problems, in the name of Jesus.

14. I command every demon in-charge of my case to go, in the name of Jesus. (*See* Matthew 8:28-32).

15. Let God's special touch for my deliverance take place now, in the name of Jesus. (*See* Matthew 14:35-36).

16. I command every evil presence in my home to disappear, in the name of Jesus.

17. Every stubborn demon in my life, I rebuke you, in the name of Jesus. (*See* Matthew 17:14-18).

18. O Lord, arise and heal me by Your power, in the name of Jesus. (*See* Matthew 19:2)

19. I lay my hand upon my life for my immediate deliverance, in the name of Jesus. (*See* Mark 6:4-6).

20. Every evil voice that is speaking against my deliverance, be silenced, in the name of Jesus. (*See* Mark 1:23-29).

21. Every dead aspect of my destiny, receive abundant life, in the name of Jesus. (*See* Acts 9:36-43).

22. Every enemy of my complete deliverance, fail woefully, in the name of Jesus.

23. I command every part of my life to discharge demons in them now, in the name of Jesus.

24. You, my life, receive complete deliverance now, in the name of Jesus.

Chapter TWO

WARFARE PRAYERS SECTION

CHAPTER OVERVIEW

Prayers in this section include prayers to overcome drug addiction, avoid criminal records, outlive death threats, overcome destructive habits, fearful intimidating problems, frustrations, deal with kidnappers and overcome evil habits.

PRAYER TOPICS ON THIS SECTION

PRAYER TO OVERCOME DRUG ADDICTION

Addiction to harmful drugs is one of the chief death traps for young people. That's why many youths are in bondage all over the world. Most of them are confused and cannot help themselves any longer.

> *"For we know that the law is spiritual: but I am carnal, sold under sin. For that which I do I allow not: for what I would, that do I not; but what I hate, that do I. If then I do that which I would not, I consent unto the law that it is good. Now then it is no more I that do it, but sin that dwelleth in me. For I know that in me (that is, in my flesh,) dwelleth no good thing: for to will is present with me; but how to perform that which is good I find not. For the good that I would I do not: but the evil which I would not, that I do"* (Romans 7:14-19).

The purpose of these prayers is to help people, especially youths, trapped into drug addiction to be free. People, who are obsessed with drugs or possessed by the spirit of addiction, can regain freedom through the name of Jesus. Therefore, I cast out any evil spirit that has put you in slavery and bondage. If you are addicted to any drug or food, I declare your freedom now in the name of Jesus.

> *"The LORD shall make the pestilence cleave unto thee, until he have consumed thee from off the land, whither thou goest to possess it. The LORD shall smite thee with a consumption, and with a fever, and with an inflammation, and with an extreme burning, and with the sword, and with blasting, and with mildew; and*

they shall pursue thee until thou perish" (<u>Deuteronomy 28:21-22</u>).

"The LORD will smite thee with the botch of Egypt, and with the emerods, and with the scab, and with the itch, whereof thou canst not be healed. The LORD shall smite thee with madness, and blindness, and astonishment of heart" (<u>Deuteronomy 28:27-28</u>).

True deliverance by the name of Jesus means uprooting evil seeds, becoming free from spells, curses and jinxes.

PRAYER POINTS

1. I break and loose myself from the yoke of evil consumption, in the name of Jesus.

2. Father Lord, deliver me from the bondage of drug addiction, in the name of Jesus.

3. Every yoke of smoking in my life, break, in the name of Jesus.

4. I command every desire for drugs in my life to die, in the name of Jesus.

5. O Lord, arise and deliver me from spiritual slavery, in the name of Jesus.

6. Every enemy of my freedom, die, in the name of Jesus.

7. Blood of Jesus, flow into my life and destroy the spirit of addiction, in the name of Jesus.

8. Father Lord, empower me to hate drugs forever, in the name of Jesus.

9. I cast out every demon of drugs upon my life, in the name of Jesus.

10. O God, arise and chase away every witchcraft animal in my life, in the name of Jesus.

11. Any evil personality in-charge of drug addiction in my life, die, in the name of Jesus.

12. Any evil department that has vowed to waste my life with drugs, scatter in desolation, in the name of Jesus.

13. I withdraw my name from the list of drug addicts, in the name of Jesus.

14. Every unclean spirit that is living inside me, come out and die, in the name of Jesus.

15. O Lord, deliver me from evil influences, in the name of Jesus.

16. Any friend or enemy encouraging me to take drugs, I reject you and your drugs, in the name of Jesus.

17. Father Lord, deliver me from evil gangs, in the name of Jesus.

18. Heavenly Father, destroy my desires for drugs, in the name of Jesus.

19. Let the sight of drugs irritate me from today, in the name of Jesus.

PRAYER TO AVOID CRIMINAL RECORDS

In deliverance, there are characters commonly referred to as prison characters. Once you notice any of these characters manifest in your life, it means either you are imprisoned spiritually or you are confined physically in some places you may not be aware of. The bible called these characters the works of the flesh.

"Now the works of the flesh are manifest, which are these; Adultery, fornication, uncleanness, lasciviousness, Idolatry, witchcraft, hatred, variance, emulations, wrath, strife, seditions, heresies, Envyings, murders, drunkenness, revellings, and such like: of the which I tell you before, as I have also told you in time past, that they which do such things shall not inherit the kingdom of God" (Galatians 5:19-21).

"For we know that the law is spiritual: but I am carnal, sold under sin. For that which I do I allow not: for what I would, that do I not; but what I hate, that do I. If then I do that which I would not, I consent unto the law that it is good. Now then it is no more I that do it, but sin that dwelleth in me. For I know that in me (that is, in my flesh,) dwelleth no good thing: for to will is present with me; but how to perform that which is good I find not. For the good that I would I do not: but the evil which I would not, that I do. Now if I do that I would not, it is no more I that do it, but sin that dwelleth in me. I find then a law, that, when I would do good, evil is present with me. For I delight in the law of God after the inward man: But I see another law in my members, warring against the law of my mind,

and bringing me into captivity to the law of sin which is in my members. O wretched man that I am! who shall deliver me from the body of this death?" (Romans 7:14-24)

Works of the flesh have forced many greatly destined people to lead useless lives. More so, it is possible that people, who possess these characters, can attack incessantly, even when you do not possess them. But you are protected by the grace of the Most High God, as you continue in this prayer program.

"Then the presidents and princes sought to find occasion against Daniel concerning the kingdom; but they could find none occasion nor fault; forasmuch as he was faithful, neither was there any error or fault found in him. Then said these men, We shall not find any occasion against this Daniel, except we find it against him concerning the law of his God" (Daniel 6:4-5).

"Then the king commanded, and they brought Daniel, and cast him into the den of lions. Now the king spake and said unto Daniel, Thy God whom thou servest continually, he will deliver thee" (Daniel 6:16).

Pray against the works of the flesh and against agents of Satan. Criminal records would have nothing to do with when you live in the spirit. That's when God fights against people, who conspire together to destroy you.

"Then these presidents and princes assembled together to the king, and said thus unto him, King Darius, live forever. All the presidents of the kingdom, the governors, and the princes, the counselors, and the captains, have consulted together to establish a royal statute, and to make a firm decree, that whosoever

shall ask a petition of any God or man for thirty days, save of thee, O king, he shall be cast into the den of lions. Now, O king, establish the decree, and sign the writing, that it be not changed, according to the law of the Medes and Persians, which altereth not. Wherefore king Darius signed the writing and the decree. Now when Daniel knew that the writing was signed, he went into his house; and his windows being open in his chamber toward Jerusalem, he kneeled upon his knees three times a day, and prayed, and gave thanks before his God, as he did aforetime. Then these men assembled, and found Daniel praying and making supplication before his God. Then they came near, and spake before the king concerning the king's decree; Hast thou not signed a decree, that every man that shall ask a petition of any God or man within thirty days, save of thee, O king, shall be cast into the den of lions? The king answered and said, The thing is true, according to the law of the Medes and Persians, which altered not. Then answered they and said before the king, That Daniel, which is of the children of the captivity of Judah, regarded not thee, O king, nor the decree that thou hast signed, but maketh his petition three times a day. Then the king, when he heard these words, was sore displeased with himself, and set his heart on Daniel to deliver him: and he labored till the going down of the sun to deliver him. Then these men assembled unto the king, and said unto the king, Know, O king, that the law of the Medes and Persians is, That no decree nor statute which the king established may be changed. Then the king commanded, and they brought Daniel, and cast him into the den of lions. Now the king spake and said unto Daniel, Thy God whom thou servest continually, he will deliver thee. And a stone was brought, and laid upon the mouth of the den; and the king sealed it with his own signet, and with the signet of his lords; that the purpose might not be changed concerning Daniel" (<u>Daniel 6:6-17</u>).

PRAYER POINTS

1. O Lord, forgive me for involving myself in any sort of crime in the past, in the name of Jesus.

2. Let the mercy of God fall upon me now, in the name of Jesus.

3. I break and loose myself from consequences of my past sins, in the name of Jesus.

4. Let heaven wipe away any criminal records recorded for my sake, in the name of Jesus.

5. O Lord, blot out all my sins from Your sight, in the name of Jesus.

6. Blood of Jesus, deliver me from criminal records spiritually, in the name of Jesus.

7. Every enemy against my excellent life, die, in the name of Jesus.

8. Father Lord, deliver me from various forms of defilement and pollution, in the name of Jesus.

9. I delete every evil record stored against me, in the name of Jesus.

10. Any criminal record that was designed to make me useless, fail woefully, in the name of Jesus.

11. Lord Jesus, restore my spirit and take away counterfeit spirit, in the name of Jesus.

12. Any evil kingdom in-charge of my case, scatter in shame, in the name of Jesus.

13. Any evil spirit assigned to publish criminal records for my sake, be paralyzed, in the name of Jesus.

14. I deliver myself from common problems attached to people with criminal records, in the name of Jesus.

15. O Lord, help me to make it without being limited by criminal records, in the name of Jesus.

16. I reject any bad name given to me because of criminal records, in the name of Jesus.

17. O Lord, give me an establishment that will advertise my talents, in the name of Jesus.

18. Father Lord, bless and prosper me greatly, in the name of Jesus.

19. I receive the spirit of excellence, in the name of Jesus.

20. O Lord, show me where to cast my nets on earth, in the name of Jesus.

21. Any spirit of inferiority complex in me, come out and die, in the name of Jesus.

22. O Lord, cancel any criminal record written for my sake, in the name of Jesus.

PRAYER TO OUTLIVE DEATH THREATS

Are you one of those people living under outrageous threats to your life? Fear not, for the Lord is with you. Millions of people are living under the threats of deaths. While others are malicious threats, others are polite. When your doctor informs you of your imminent death, you cannot afford to plan for your obituary immediately. You can trust God to reverse the doctor's verdict.

> *"In those days was Hezekiah sick unto death. And Isaiah the prophet the son of Amoz came unto him, and said unto him, Thus saith the LORD, Set thine house in order: for thou shalt die, and not live. Then Hezekiah turned his face toward the wall, and prayed unto the LORD, And said, Remember now, O LORD, I beseech thee, how I have walked before thee in truth and with a perfect heart, and have done that which is good in thy sight. And Hezekiah wept sore"* (<u>Isaiah 38:1-3</u>).

Hezekiah turned to God in prayers when Isaiah the prophet informed him of his death. Unfortunately, verdicts of death are hanging on many people's heads today and yet they are not doing anything about it. They have not considered running to God to deliver them. When Mary and Martha saw that their only brother Lazarus was dying, they invited Jesus to remedy the situation immediately.

> *"Now a certain man was sick, named Lazarus, of Bethany, the town of Mary and her sister Martha. (It was that Mary which anointed the Lord with ointment, and wiped his feet with her hair, whose*

brother Lazarus was sick.) Therefore his sisters sent unto him, saying, Lord, behold, he whom thou lovest is sick" (John 11:1-3).

"Then said Jesus unto them plainly, Lazarus is dead" (John 11:14).

"And when he thus had spoken, he cried with a loud voice, Lazarus, come forth. And he that was dead came forth, bound hand and foot with grave clothes: and his face was bound about with a napkin. Jesus saith unto them, Loose him, and let him go" (John 11:43-44).

Death gives way when challenged in the name of Jesus.

PRAYER POINTS

1. Any sign of death in my life, I destroy you by force, in the name of Jesus.

2. O Lord, transfer every threat of death to their owners, in the name of Jesus.

3. Every arrow of death fired at my life, I fire you back, in the name of Jesus.

4. Blood of Jesus, speak destruction to every evil voice against me, in the name of Jesus.

5. Let movements of death in my life be stopped now, in the name of Jesus.

6. Every seed of death planted in my life, die by force, in the name of Jesus.

7. O Lord, arise and deliver me from the judgment of death, in the name of Jesus.

8. Every messenger of death sent against me, carry back your message to your sender, in the name of Jesus.

9. Blood of Jesus, flow into my foundation and kill every spirit of death planted therein, in the name of Jesus.

10. Any sickness assigned to kill me, I command you to die, in the name of Jesus.

11. Any evil visitor against me from the grave, die, in the name of Jesus.

12. I walk out from every trap of death to meet the prince of peace, in the name of Jesus.

13. Any coffin that was prepared against my life, catch fire, in the name of Jesus.

14. Whoever has vowed to kill me shall die for my sake, in the name of Jesus.

15. I refuse to answer any call from graveyards, in the name of Jesus.

16. Wherever death is calling me from, blood of Jesus, answer for me, in the name of Jesus.

17. Any dream of death for me, I reverse you by force, in the name of Jesus.

18. Every satanic roadblock mounted by the spirit of death against me, be dismantled, in the name of Jesus.

19. Every good thing that death has stolen from me, I recover you now, in the name of Jesus.

20. I command angels of death that were assigned to kill me to kill their senders instead, in the name of Jesus.

PRAYER TO OVERCOME DESTRUCTIVE HABITS

Bad habits can be very destructive. Surely, bad habits are works of the devil that demand urgent attention. Satan knows how to darken people's minds and reason to put up with evil habits. That's why I maintained that spirits behind bad habits are desperately wicked and deceitful. They defile people's minds and consciences, and enslave their wills (*See* Romans 7:14-24).

Spirit of evil works is one with carnal mind. Satan is a dominating tyrant, who is desperately wicked. He labors day and night to corrupt morally upright people and dehumanize them as slaves. Satan knows how to turn his slaves into traitors, outcasts, captives, lepers and enemies of God. But thanks to our Lord Jesus, who has empowered us over Satan and all his demons.

> *"I thank God through Jesus Christ our Lord. So then with the mind I myself serve the law of God; but with the flesh the law of sin"* (Romans 7:25).

> *"Come unto me, all ye that labor and are heavy laden, and I will give you rest. Take my yoke upon you, and learn of me; for I am meek and lowly in heart: and ye shall find rest unto your souls. For my yoke is easy, and my burden is light"* (Mathew 11:28-30).

Paul, Daniel, Joseph, etc., all fought one form of evil habit or another, and overcame them. You can also overcome any form of evil habit when you repent and pray.

PRAYER POINTS

1. Every chain of bad habit in my life, break, in the name of Jesus.

2. Blood of Jesus, flow into the root of my life and destroy the spirit of bad habit, in the name of Jesus.

3. Let every spirit of wastage in my character be dragged out and destroyed, in the name of Jesus.

4. I command the fire of God to burn every root of iniquity in my life, in the name of Jesus.

5. Every evil desire in my life, come out, in the name of Jesus.

6. Blood of Jesus, eliminate every evil habit in every area of my life, in the name of Jesus.

7. Let every evil habit I inherited from my ancestors be uprooted, in the name of Jesus.

8. Let the stronghold of bad habits in my life collapse, in the name of Jesus.

9. Any evil power infesting my life with bad habits, be blinded, in the name of Jesus.

10. Father Lord, plant in me the tree of righteousness, in the name of Jesus.

11. I command the strongman of sin in my life to fall down and die, in the name of Jesus.

12. Father Lord, impute your righteousness in me by fire, in the name of Jesus.

13. Any serpent of bad habit in my life, die, in the name of Jesus.

14. Every poison of bad habit in my life, dry up by fire, in the name of Jesus.

15. I soak my life in the blood of Jesus for purity, in the name of Jesus.

16. Every agent of sin in my life, die, in the name of Jesus.

17. Any spirit of bad character that was programmed into my life, come out and die, in the name of Jesus.

18. Angels of righteousness, plant righteousness in my life, in the name of Jesus.

19. I send the consuming fire of God against evil habits in my foundation, in the name of Jesus.

20. I refuse to remain under the bondage of any bad habit, in the name of Jesus.

21. O Lord, arise and destroy bad habits in my life, in the name of Jesus.

22. Heavenly Father, break every bondage of bad habit in my life, in the name of Jesus.

23. Fire of God, burn every weapon of bad habit in my life, in the name of Jesus.

24. Bad habit, you will not harvest my life, in the name of Jesus.

25. Let the power of God create righteousness in me, in the name of Jesus.

26. O Lord, plant the fruits of Your Spirit in the garden of my life, in the name of Jesus.

27. Every destroyer of good things in my foundation, be roasted by fire, in the name of Jesus.

28. Every product of bad habit in my life, die, in the name of Jesus.

29. Let the engine of evil things in my life become damaged, in the name of Jesus.

30. Holy Ghost fire, consume every evil in my life, in the name of Jesus.

31. Every stone of bad habit in my life, melt by fire, in the name of Jesus.

32. Father Lord, destroy every material of bad habit in my life, in the name of Jesus.

33. Any power corrupting my life, catch fire, in the name of Jesus.

34. I command the witchcraft of bad habit in my life to die, in the name of Jesus.

35. Let the throne of witchcraft in my life collapse now, in the name of Jesus.

36. Every force of bad habit in my life, scatter by force, in the name of Jesus.

37. Any evil personality, promoting bad habit in my life, be disgraced, in the name of Jesus.

38. I release my life from the yoke of bad habits, in the name of Jesus.

39. Any evil character controlling my life, die, in the name of Jesus.

40. Any foundational strongman attacking me with bad habits, die, in the name of Jesus.

41. O Lord, arise in Your power and crucify bad habit in my life, in the name of Jesus.

42. Blood of Jesus, flush out every manner of bad habit in my life, in the name of Jesus.

43. Let the powers of darkness introducing bad habit in my life die, in the name of Jesus.

44. I command the ministry of bad habit in my life to be terminated, in the name of Jesus.

45. Any voice of bad habit in my life, be silenced forever, in the name of Jesus.

46. O Lord, give me power to live above bad habits, in the name of Jesus.

47. Every strange character in my life, die, in the name of Jesus.

48. Any power from the marine kingdom attacking my life, die, in the name of Jesus.

49. Every water spirit character in my life, die by force, in the name of Jesus.

50. Heavenly Father, plant in me a heavenly habit, in the name of Jesus.

51. Every enemy of holiness in my life, die, in the name of Jesus.

52. Any power from the waters that is assigned to corrupt my life, die, in the name of Jesus.

53. Lord Jesus, deliver me from the grip of marine powers, in the name of Jesus.

54. Fire of God, burn every trace of marine deposit in my life, in the name of Jesus.

PRAYER AGAINST FEARFUL AND INTIMIDATING PROBLEMS

There have been cases where fearful and easily intimidated people claim to hear terrible voices. Sometimes, these voices are voices of intimidating problems echoing in people's ears. They strive to diminish people's hope and confidence in God, as they bombard their minds with negative and fearful reports. These protracted evil voices are often what lead most people to accept defeats and surrender to devil's will.

> *"In those days was Hezekiah sick unto death. And Isaiah the prophet the son of Amoz came unto him, and said unto him, Thus saith the LORD, Set thine house in order: for thou shalt die, and not live"* (Isaiah 38:1).

> *"And he stood and cried unto the armies of Israel, and said unto them, Why are ye come out to set your battle in array? Am not I a Philistine, and ye servants to Saul? Choose you a man for you, and let him come down to me. If he be able to fight with me, and to kill me, then will we be your servants: but if I prevail against him, and kill him, then shall ye be our servants, and serve us. And the Philistine said, I defy the armies of Israel this day; give me a man, that we may fight together. When Saul and all Israel heard those words of the Philistine, they were dismayed, and greatly afraid"* (1 Samuel 17:8-11).

You have to challenge evil voices of intimidating problems with prayers. You cannot afford to allow them to continue pursuing you away from your destiny. Otherwise, their consistent and wicked torments can lead to spiritual or physical death.

> "In *whom the god of this world hath blinded the minds of them which believe not, lest the light of the glorious gospel of Christ, who is the image of God, should shine unto them*" (2 Corinthians 4:4).

> "*They that see thee shall narrowly look upon thee, and consider thee, saying, Is this the man that made the earth to tremble, that did shake kingdoms; That made the world as a wilderness, and destroyed the cities thereof; that opened not the house of his prisoners?*" (Isaiah 14:16-17).

Recall that Noah confronted and conquered similar voices of fear and intimidation from the people. Hannah also triumphed over them. Hezekiah subdued them (*See* Isaiah 38:1-5). Therefore, you can also do the same successfully. Rise and confront intimidating and fearful voices tormenting your life with these prayers.

PRAYER POINTS

1. I silence every voice of Goliath that is still crying into my ears, in the name of Jesus.

2. I command any strongman targeting my life to become impotent, in the name of Jesus.

3. Any problem that is sponsoring failure into my life, die by fire, in the name of Jesus.

4. I destroy any destructive fear that is tormenting my life, in the name of Jesus.

5. Let all impossible things in my life become possible by force, in the name of Jesus.

6. Every enemy of my breakthrough, wherever you are, die, in the name of Jesus.

7. Blood of Jesus, speak death to all my problems, in the name of Jesus.

8. I command every determined enemy of my destiny to die, in the name of Jesus.

9. I frustrate any Egyptian army pursuing my life and I command them to scatter and die, in the name of Jesus.

10. Let the Red Sea ahead of me begin to divide immediately, in the name of Jesus.

11. I pull down every wall of Jericho standing against my life, in the name of Jesus.

12. O Lord, arise and defeat my enemies, in the name of Jesus.

13. Any wicked voice that is ridiculing my life, I silence you to death, in the name of Jesus.

14. I command every stronghold of the devil in my life to collapse, in the name of Jesus.

15. Any giant in my promise land, die, in the name of Jesus.

16. Let every spirit of Herod that has decided to disgrace me be disgrace, in the name of Jesus.

17. Any witch or wizard that has vowed to destroy my life, be destroyed, in the name of Jesus.

18. Any wickedness targeting to destroy my life, destroy your sender, in the name of Jesus.

19. Every weapon of darkness provided to destroy me, catch fire, in the name of Jesus.

20. Let every evil altar militating against my life catch fire, in the name of Jesus.

21. I break and loose myself from destructive covenant and curses, in the name of Jesus.

22. I cancel all enchantment and curse designed to waste my life, in the name of Jesus.

23. Any evil kingdom standing against God in my life, be subdued by fire, in the name of Jesus.

24. Any evil gathering assigned to terminate my life, scatter in shame, in the name of Jesus.

25. O Lord, arise and take me away from poverty to prosperity, in the name of Jesus.

26. Any determined oppressor that has vowed to oppress me, die, in the name of Jesus.

27. I receive power to put fear into my problems, in the name of Jesus.

PRAYER TO OVERCOME FRUSTRATIONS

Curse is one of the most dangerous weapons that devil uses to frustrate people. A curse is like a legal document that enforces a decree or a will. That's why when any curse is operating in someone's life, frustration continues to take toll in such person's life.

> "And Joshua made them that day hewers of wood and drawers of water for the congregation, and for the altar of the LORD, even unto this day, in the place which he should choose" (Joshua 9:27).

> "The leprosy therefore of Naaman shall cleave unto thee, and unto thy seed forever. And he went out from his presence a leper as white as snow" (2 Kings 5:27).

Curse is direct opposite of blessing. It fights against every sight of blessing in its victim's life. That's why you need to pray fervently to overcome any trace of curse operating in your life. It could be an evil wish, an utterance or evil words put together to torment you or your entire family.

Any wise person cannot treat curses lightly or nonchalantly because curses are capable of frustrating people to struggle in life without achievements. Like spell or jinx, curses limit people greatly and stand as barriers between them and good things. They can manifest in forms of non-achievement, hatred, rejection, bad luck or the almost-there syndrome in the quest for good things of life.

Curses can manipulate one to borrow, beg and meet with the wrong people. Christians, who desire to enjoy the goodness of God in their lives, should pray against curses and frustrations.

PRAYER POINTS

1.   I destroy every attack that is making me to get tired of life, in the name of Jesus.

2.   I frustrate every agent of frustration that is after my life, in the name of Jesus.

3.   Blood of Jesus, terminate my frustrations, in the name of Jesus.

4.   Whatever frustration has destroyed in my life, receive resurrection, in the name of Jesus.

5.   Every arrow of frustration from the waters fired at my life, backfire, in the name of Jesus.

6.   Every marine chain of frustration, break, in the name of Jesus.

7.   Every embargo of the queen of heaven placed upon my life to frustrate me, die, in the name of Jesus.

8.   Any evil cloud gathered by leviathan to frustrate me, scatter, in the name of Jesus.

9.   Let all troublemakers of my father's house that are frustrating me be disgraced, in the name of Jesus.

10. Lord Jesus, arise and frustrate all my stubborn enemies, in the name of Jesus.

11. Any evil inheritance from water spirits that is frustrating my life, die, in the name of Jesus.

12. Heavenly father, send Your comfort from heaven for my sake, in the name of Jesus.

13. Wherever my frustration is coming from, O Lord, deliver me, in the name of Jesus.

14. Any evil pattern in my family that wants to frustrate me, die in shame, in the name of Jesus.

15. Every agent of frustration that is following me about, be frustrated, in the name of Jesus.

16. Every yoke of frustration placed upon my life, break by fire, in the name of Jesus.

17. Father Lord, destroy every frustration from water spirits, in the name of Jesus.

18. Let the kingdom of the queen of the coast in my life collapse, in the name of Jesus.

19. Fire of God, burn every weapon of frustration upon my life to ashes, in the name of Jesus.

20. Any demonic plan to kill my ambitions with frustration, be exposed, in the name of Jesus.

21. Any frustration going on secretly to waste my destiny, die, in the name of Jesus.

22. Heavenly Father, arise and deliver me from marine spirit attacks, in the name of Jesus.

23. I reject every marine spirits' gifts designed to frustrate me, in the name of Jesus.

24. Every yoke of lack in any area of my life that has been assigned to frustrate me, break, in the name of Jesus.

25. Every water spirit of hindrance to my promotion, clear away by force, in the name of Jesus.

26. Let altars of darkness that are receiving sacrifices to frustrate me catch fire, in the name of Jesus.

27. Every stronghold of poverty in my family that was built to frustrate my efforts, collapse, in the name of Jesus.

28. Let mountains of frustrations against my life give way by force, in the name of Jesus.

29. Any satanic roadblock standing against my progress, be dismantled, in the name of Jesus.

30. Let ugly feet of frustrations that have walked into my life walk out by force, in the name of Jesus.

31. Altars of frustration that was built for my sake, scatter in disgrace, in the name of Jesus.

32. I command every garment of frustration in my life to catch fire and burn to ashes, in the name of Jesus.

33. Every witchcraft animal assigned to frustrate my sleep and peace, die, in the name of Jesus.

34. Any evil power, bringing frustration into my business, be frustrated, in the name of Jesus.

35. Every river of frustration channeled against me, be diverted by force, in the name of Jesus.

36. Let every serpentine poison in my body dry up, in the name of Jesus.

37. Every root of frustration in my life, be uprooted, in the name of Jesus.

38. Anointing to destroy all manner of frustrations, fall upon me, in the name of Jesus.

39. Every demonic angel of frustration, be frustrated, in the name of Jesus.

40. Any tree of frustration that is planted in my life, dry up, in

the name of Jesus.

41. Blood of Jesus, enter into the waters for my sake and destroy frustrations, in the name of Jesus.

42. Let the entire household enemies against my peace fall for my sake, in the name of Jesus.

43. Any dragon of my father's house that is working hard to frustrate me, die, in the name of Jesus.

44. Queen of the coast, you will never frustrate me, in the name of Jesus.

45. I fire back to the waters every arrow of frustration fired at my life, in the name of Jesus.

46. Lord Jesus, give me power to live above marine frustrations, in the name of Jesus.

47. My eagle, fly above every marine spirit's plan of frustration, in the name of Jesus.

PRAYER TO DEAL WITH KIDNAPPERS

A kidnapper is somebody who takes somebody else away by force or deception. Just like people can be kidnapped physically, people can also be kidnapped spiritually. Destinies of many people have been kidnapped and are waiting for total ruin. Pray these prayers to deal with spiritual and physical kidnappers.

> *"Saying, where is he that is born king of the Jews? For we have seen his star in the east, and are come to worship him... When they had heard the king, they departed; and, lo, the star, which they saw in the east, went before them, till it came and stood over where the young child was"* (Matthew 2:2, 9).

> *"And when it was day, certain of the Jews banded together, and bound themselves under a curse, saying that they would neither eat nor drink till they had killed Paul. [13]And they were more than forty which had made this conspiracy"* (Acts 23:12-13).

When evil people kidnap your destiny and you chose to do nothing about it, then your problems are likely to multiply exceedingly. Captured stars of many people are now waiting for execution. The wise men from the east must have prayed as they followed the star of Jesus, for they understood the significance of stars.

Increasingly, satanic agents are seeking to capture people's stars. Equally, many have been arrested already and their kidnappers are demanding for unreasonable ransom for their heads.

61

PRAYER POINTS

1. Every evil movement toward me, stop, in the name of Jesus.

2. I paralyze evil messengers sent to kidnap me, in the name of Jesus.

3. Any spiritual force that has arrested me spiritually, release me by force, in the name of Jesus.

4. Any evil decision against my life, be exposed and be disappointed, in the name of Jesus.

5. Any evil plan to kidnap me, be aborted, in the name of Jesus.

6. Every plan or plot to kidnap me, be revealed by mistake, in the name of Jesus.

7. Let secrets of my enemies be made open mysteriously, in the name of Jesus.

8. I demobilize my kidnappers mobility by fire, in the name of Jesus.

9. I command confusion to arise in the midst of my kidnappers, in the name of Jesus.

10. Let my kidnappers become confused, in the name of Jesus.

11. Let my kidnappers begin to quarrel among themselves, in the name of Jesus.

12. Every weapon of death that my kidnappers carry, destroy your owners, in the name of Jesus.

13. I command every evil gathering against me to scatter in shame, in the name of Jesus.

14. Father Lord, help me to find favor before my kidnappers, in the name of Jesus.

15. Let my unfriendly friends be exposed and disgraced, in the name of Jesus.

16. Let the wind of disagreement blow into the camp of my kidnappers, in the name of Jesus.

17. O Lord, deliver me from the hands of my kidnappers, in the name of Jesus.

18. Let destructive fear of God overpower my kidnappers, in the name of Jesus.

19. I scatter the brains of my kidnappers and command madness upon them, in the name of Jesus.

20. Let my kidnappers decide to my favor, in the name of Jesus.

21. Let my kidnappers receive double destruction by force, in the name of Jesus.

22. Father Lord, deliver me miraculously from the activities of kidnappers, in the name of Jesus.

PRAYER TO OVERCOME EVIL HABITS

Evil habits have ruined many people's lives. However, the worst evil habit that can hold any man or woman on earth is sin. Sadly, most people are still underestimating the consequences of evil habits. But my prayer is that no evil habit will destroy you in Jesus name.

> *"[19]For the good that I would I do not: but the evil which I would not, that I do... [21]I find then a law, that, when I would do good, evil is present with me. [22]For I delight in the law of God after the inward man: [23]But I see another law in my members, warring against the law of my mind, and bringing me into captivity to the law of sin which is in my members. [24]O wretched man that I am! who shall deliver me from the body of this death?"* (Romans 7:19, 21-24).

Many people are addicted to evil habit of smoking, drinking, sexual lust and drugs of all kinds. However, the most destructive is the habit of sin, which is a great enemy against God.

> *"[25]I thank God through Jesus Christ our Lord. So then with the mind I myself serve the law of God; but with the flesh the law of sin"* (Romans 7:25).

Paul wrote in thanksgiving to God for using the power of Christ to set him free. When you surrender your life to Christ as you pray these prayers, Jesus is able to deliver you perfectly.

PRAYER POINTS

1. Every yoke of bad habit in my life, break to pieces, in the name of Jesus.

2. Fire of God, uproot the root of bad habits in my life by fire, in the name of Jesus.

3. Let great earthquake of God destroy evil habits in my life, in the name of Jesus.

4. Let the destroying flood of God deliver me from evil habits, in the name of Jesus.

5. Let every bad character in my life receive shock and die, in the name of Jesus.

6. Any satanic bondage in my life, break to pieces, in the name of Jesus.

7. Forces of darkness that is protecting my problems, scatter in shame, in the name of Jesus.

8. I command destruction upon every problem in my life, in the name of Jesus.

9. Any problem that is attacking me from the air, receive air quake, in the name of Jesus.

10. Every bad habit in my life, receive earthquake and die, in the name of Jesus.

11. Holy Ghost fire, burn the power of bad habits in my life, in the name of Jesus.

12. Let the flood of God carry away the strength of evil habits from my life, in the name of Jesus.

13. Any bad habit that has vowed to destroy me, receive bitter destruction, in the name of Jesus.

14. Blood of Jesus, eliminate the strongman of evil habit in my life, in the name of Jesus.

15. Let the worm eat up evil habits in my life, in the name of Jesus.

16. You, bad habits in my life, die by unbearable heat of God, in the name of Jesus.

17. You, stronghold of evil habits in my life, I cut off your head, die, in the name of Jesus.

18. Any arrow of bad habit in my life, I fire you back, in the name of Jesus.

19. Any serpent of bad habit in my life, die by force, in the name of Jesus.

20. Owners of evil load of bad habits in my life, carry your load, in the name of Jesus.

21. Father Lord, deliver me from bad habits, in the name of Jesus.

Other titles in this series – ALONE WITH GOD

1. ## Prayers for Good Health

Prayers in this series include prayers to overcome asthma, diabetes, high blood pressure, surgeries, cancer, brain tumor, ectopic and prolong pregnancies, facial disease, fibroid and evil plantations, heart enlargement, incurable diseases, insanity, mental illness, sleeplessness, ulcers, heart disease, safe delivery, strokes, kidney problem, pneumonia, fever, poison, demonic burns, dog bite poisons, diarrhea, epilepsy, toothache and breast lump.

2. ## Prayers for Financial Breakthrough

Prayers in this series include prayers for financial assistance, finance breakthrough, financial miracles, divine breakthrough and opportunities, divine connections, business breakthrough, divine promotion, prosperity, protection from enemies, protection from evil, deliverance from poverty, overcoming enemies in the place of work, paying bills, prospering in business, divine connections, prospering in foreign land, recovering lost businesses, recovering a lost job, recovering all your loss, reviving collapsed or collapsing business, revoking evil decrees, rise from defeat, searching and finding jobs, stopping determined enemies, succeeding where others are failing and prayers to survive economic meltdown/famine.

3. ## Prayers for Marriage & Family

Prayers in this series deal with attacks at home, polygamous spirit, eating and having sex in dreams, having sex outside marriage, sexual weaknesses among legally married couples, broken homes, husbands who experience hatred from their wives, people who become sexually active with outsiders only, people who become sexually weak before their spouse, families in distress, men who are captured by strange women, true friendship, a godly woman, men who are sexually disconnected from their wives, women who experience hatred from their husbands, women who trust God for a child at old age, bear godly children, end a spirit marriage, become fertile and productive, deliver your children, frustrate divorce plans, keep your pregnancy, prevent miscarriage, end prolonged pregnancy, end separation plans, stop the enemies of your marriage and prayers to overcome troubles in your marriage.

4. Prayers against Satanic Oppression

Prayers in this series include prayers for protection from evil spirits, overcoming hopelessness, against all odds, arrows in the dream, attacks on churches, bewitchment, the spirit of confusion, marine curses, marine covenants, natural disasters, opposition at the work place, destroyers of environments, attacks in the dream, graveyard spirits, the power of sin, unknown enemies, overturn your defeats, disengage evil partners, overcome stress, crush witchcraft attacks, cross over to the next level, close witchcraft doors, cast out sexual demons, cast out demon of epilepsy and prayers to burn satanic liabilities.

5. Prayers for Children & Youth

Prayers in this series include prayers for bachelors and spinsters, before birthday, 3 days prayer for school children, children whose parents are divorced, victory at all cost, young school children, youths and teenagers, train children well.

6. Prayers for Overcoming Attitude Problems

Prayers in this series include prayers to overcome drug addiction, avoid criminal records, outlive death threats, overcome destructive habits, overcome fearful and intimidating problems, frustrations, deal with kidnappers and prayers to overcome evil habits.

7. Prayers for Academic Success

Prayers in this section include prayers for success in examination, prayers before examination, during examination, after examination, prayers for breakthrough in examination, prayers before an interview and prayer for undergraduates.

8. Prayers for A Successful Career

Prayers in this series include prayers to keep your job and destiny, for footballers, career people, for great and immediate changes, for guidance, new job, for sportsmen and women, best employment, to be self or gainfully employed, for a better job, enter into a new place, excel above your masters, excel in a job interview, force your enemies out of comfort, force your enemies to bow, move God into action, open closed doors, unburden your burdens and prayer to win in competitions.

9. Prayers for Deliverance

Prayers in this series include prayers for deliverance, against evil marks, evil traditions, for family tree, break the seal of bondage, break the yoke of death, destroy evil delays, destroy evil movements in the body, destroy serpents in the body, against your sinful pasts, for peace of mind, total freedom, stop the wicked, stop future enemies

10. Special Prayers in His Presence

Prayers in this series include prayers to win court, hospital and police cases, prayer at new year eves, for Africa, blessings, citizenship, cleansing, comfort, compassion, confidence, courage, Good Friday, Easter Sunday morning, Easter Saturday, encouragement, journey mercies, fellowship, ministry, to be touched for Christ, for residence permits, right decisions, safety, security, sponsorship, United Nations, Valentine's day, to be selected among the eleven, to preserve America and prayers to overcome all unknown problems.

11. <u>Alone With God (Complete version)</u> – This is the complete version of the ten-part series of ALONE WITH GOD. This book can be a highly resourceful prayer companion in your libraries and prayer ministries.

Thank You So Much!

Beloved, I hope you enjoyed this book as much as I believe God has touched your heart today. I cannot thank you enough for your continued support for this prayer ministry.

I appreciate you so much for taking out time to read this wonderful prayer book, and if you have an extra second, I would love to hear what you think about this book.

Please, do share your testimonies with me by sending an email to me at pastor@prayermadueke.com, or in Facebook at www.facebook.com/prayer.madueke. I personally invite you also to my website at *www.prayermadueke.com* to view many other books I have written on various issues of life, especially on marriage, family, sexual problems and money.

I will be delighted to partner with you in organized crusades, ceremonies, marriages and Marriage seminars, special events, church ministration and fellowship for the advancement of God's Kingdom here on earth.

Thank you again, and I wish you nothing less than success in life.

God bless you.

Prayer M. Madueke

OTHER BOOKS BY PRAYER M. MADUEKE

- *21/40 Nights Of Decrees And Your Enemies Will Surrender*
- *Confront And Conquer*
- *35 Special Dangerous Decrees*
- *Tears in Prison*
- *The Reality of Spirit Marriage*
- *Queen of Heaven*
- *Leviathan the Beast*
- *100 Days Prayer To Wake Up Your Lazarus*
- *Dangerous Decrees To Destroy Your Destroyers*
- *The spirit of Christmas*
- *More Kingdoms To Conquer*
- *Your Dream Directory*
- *The Sword Of New Testament Deliverance*
- *Alphabetic Battle For Unmerited Favors*
- *Alphabetic Character Deliverance*
- *Holiness*
- *The Witchcraft Of The Woman That Sits Upon Many Waters*
- *The Operations Of The Woman That Sits Upon Many Waters*
- *Powers To Pray Once And Receive Answers*
- *Prayer Riots To Overthrow Divorce*
- *Prayers To Get Married Happily*
- *Prayers To Keep Your Marriage Out of Troubles*
- *Prayers For Conception And Power To Retain*
- *Prayer Retreat – Prayers to Possess Your Year*
- *Prayers for Nation Building (Volumes 1, 2 & 3)*
- *Organized student in a disorganized school*
- *Welcome to Campus*
- *Alone with God (10 series)*

CONTACTS

AFRICA

#1 Babatunde close,
Off Olaitan Street, Surulere
Lagos, Nigeria
+234 803 353 0599
pastor@prayermadueke.com,

#28B Ubiaja Crescent
Garki II Abuja,
FCT - Nigeria
+234 807 065 4159

IRELAND

Ps Emmanuel Oko
#84 Thornfield Square
Cloudalkin D22
Ireland
Tel: +353 872 820 909, +353 872 977 422
aghaoko2003@yahoo.com

EUROPE/SCHENGEN

Collins Kwame
#46 Felton Road
Barking
Essex IG11 7XZ GB
Tel: +44 208 507 8083, +44 787 703 2386, +44 780 703 6916
aghaoko2003@yahoo.com

Printed in Great Britain
by Amazon

47406909R00047